TIPS FOR BRIDES

Asta Jakubson

Money & Stress
Saving Tips

One of
PARIS FASHION
WEEK
Award Winning Designer

5 Tips on how to:
Pick the perfect wedding dress
for your body shape!

AuthorHouse™ UK
1663 Liberty Drive
Bloomington, IN 47403 USA
www.authorhouse.co.uk
Phone: 0800 047 8203 (Domestic TFN)
+44 1908 723714 (International)

Because of the dynamic nature of the Internet, any web addresses or links contained in this book may have changed
since publication and may no longer be valid. The views expressed in this work are solely those of the author and do not
necessarily reflect the views of the publisher, and the publisher hereby disclaims any responsibility for them.

Any people depicted in stock imagery provided by Getty Images are models,
and such images are being used for illustrative purposes only.
Certain stock imagery © Getty Images.

ISBN: 978-1-7283-9225-7 (sc)
ISBN: 978-1-7283-9224-0 (e)

Library of Congress Control Number: 2019912310

Print information available on the last page.

This book is printed on acid-free paper.

Published by AuthorHouse 09/02/2019

authorHOUSE®

Tips for Brides

Asta Jakubson

 Asta Jakubson is an award winning fashion designer widely recognised, both in Ireland & internationally. She believes in empowering women to express their individual style, while wearing her designs you feel unique and elegant, thus standing out from the crowd. Teaching her clients on how to dress for their body shape for any occasion making them feel confident! She learned her business skills from the best, such as: Calvin Richard Klein, Steve Wozniak, Charlie Sheen, Mel Gibson, Jessica Simpson, Brooke Shields, Michael Douglas and Dr. Phil.

Asta Jakubson is:

Award Winning Designer (2015)

One of the chosen Paris Fashion Week Designers (2019)

After her return from Paris Fashion Week, Asta Jakubson was featured in Worldwide Fashion Magazines, such as 'Fashion Week Online', 'The Garnette Report', 'Nicole Magazine', 'Izon Magazine', 'Fashion Magazine 24', 'Fashion Maniac' among many others.

Congratulations on your engagement!

One of the first things you probably picture when envisioning your wedding is the dress!

But going through all the wedding dress shops and spending so much time and energy trying on dresses can make you frustrated. Especially when not one of them suits your body shape. You start to wonder if there's something wrong with your shape or if you should go on a diet. Maybe you don't like to shop or the shops you visit don't have what you want.

Relax, you are wonderful! Your body is amazing. Your man loves it, so you should too!

Don't panic. I am here for you! This e-book will be your personal stylist, designer, and shopping assistant. You will be able to look back on certain factors to help you choose what's best for you and your big day. It will not be just following what's trending but what actually will look great on you. And you will have amazing photos of the big day with your perfectly fitted dress to show and proudly say, "I picked this dress myself!" You don't have to tell them about me. This will be our small secret.

You just need to know some short rules before going to the shops in search of your dress.

First, you need to know what body shape you are. So which shape are you?

1. THE APPLE

You have narrow hips, a large bust, full midsection, and no waist. Your midsection is the widest part of your body.

If you have a short neck, wear V-neck. A dress with a standing collar will give that luxurious feeling and rich look. It will also make you look taller.

Note: *We have to create a waist, so broader shoulders will make it look like your waist is smaller, therefore creating more of a curve. Gathers on your waist are great to create the illusion of having a waist!*

A dress with nude panels helps to create the shape you want and gives the illusion of having a smaller waist and hips.

2. THE PEAR SHAPE

Your hips are larger than your bust. You have a defined waist, and legs are more rounded. Most likely, your slimmest parts to show are your neck and shoulders. Because your shoulders are slimmer, you need to make them look wider so they appear to be more in proportion to your hips.

A dress with nude panels helps to create the body shape you want
and give the illusion of a smaller waist.

Your wedding dress would look lovely with a peplum. We want to highlight all the wonderful features you have as a woman, and this can be done by creating curves with a peplum and the mermaid style.

3.

THE TRIANGLE

So you have broad shoulders, a wide back, and a bit more of a bust. A nice cleavage and slim legs are probably your best features, so use every opportunity to flaunt them. Wrap-style dresses are great for you.

To look a little more feminine, get some shiny belts, especially if you just want to add more details at your waist, and flurry skirts to make the rest of your body look to be in proportion with your shoulders, and your waist will look smaller.

4. THE RULER

Your shoulders and hips have the same proportion, but you have no waist. So show off your legs and bust décolleté! Big slits are very effective, and a peplum will help to make your waist look smaller. And use a belt.

Looks like a waisted jacket on the dress need to be below your hipline to create the illusion of a longer body. Don't wear a strapless dress. A small cap or any length sleeve is a must.

A V-neck dress with lots of details would look great on you. You can create your desired body shape by adding nude panels at the waistline. It will create the illusion of having an hourglass silhouette.

A boat neckline would show off your shoulders and neck nicely and create the look of a smaller waist. But if you are blessed with a larger bust, ask for a neckline a bit lower. A good dressmaker can tailor it.

5.

THE HOURGLASS

So you have a wide bust, a narrow waist and a wide hip in the same proportion, this body shape looks like a perfect curved hourglass.

If you want a belt on the dress, buy it separately. A skinny belt will not be as effective as wide one. Your hips and shoulders are in proportion with each other. A small waist is the best part of your body, so let's accentuate it as much as we can. If you like the dress, that is most important. Add your own ideas to it.

Lace boleros look great because they cover you up, and the length doesn't go below the waist. They allow you to show a bit of skin but cover the top part of your arms if you wish to.

Halter-neck dresses would look great on you too. If you are short, they add height for you. Sleeves are optional.

Let's have your legs showing. It gives a sexy and glamorous look and makes you look taller.

Now you know what to look for in your dress. But before you go to the shops for the dress, go to a good underwear department store.

Do you know that the right underwear can make you look nearly one size smaller! The right bra can add fullness or make your bust look smaller.

All these tips will help you to pick the best dress for your wonderful body. Just remember one main thing: It's your wedding; it's your big day. You have waited for this since you were a small girl, so don't let anyone—media, friends, mothers, or shop assistants—interfere with your decision.

Fashion comes and goes. What looks good on the model does not mean it will look great on you. Your body is unique and special, so make it look like it is one of the kind. Pick your wedding dress by how you feel in it and how it shows your best features. Your man loves you in any dress as long you are happy!

So best of luck shopping for your wedding dress!

If you would like to ask for my honest opinion before you pay for the dress, or if you would want to get a dress designed and made for you, or if you want alterations to your dress (only in Ireland), email me a photo showing you wearing it to astafashions@yahoo.com.

If you would like a personal e-book on how to dress for your body shape for every day, just ask in my email!

With lots of love Asta Jakubson

Printed in the United States
By Bookmasters